THE OFFICIAL
ARSENAL
ANNUAL 2015

Written by Chas Newkey-Burden
Designed by Brian Thomson

A Grange Publication

Manufactured and distributed under licence by Grange Communications Ltd., Edinburgh. Printed in the EU.

ISBN 978-1-908925-61-9

£7.99

Contents

Premier League Review 2013-14 06

Aaron Ramsey's Magic Moments 16

FA Cup Review 18

The FA Cup Final 22

10 Goals of the Season 24

Know Your History! 26

UEFA Champions League Review 28

Arsenal at the World Cup! 34

Capital One Cup Review 36

20 Facts About Per Mertesacker 38

Crossword 40

Spot the Ball 41

Player Profiles 42

Oddball Facts! 50

Junior Gunners 52

New Signings 54

The BIG Arsenal Quiz! 56

Wordsearch 58

Famous Faces 59

Anagrams 59

Competition –
Win a signed Football Shirt! 60

Quiz Answers 61

Manager's Message

Dear Supporter,

Welcome to the Official Arsenal Annual 2015.

These are exciting times for the Club. The 2013/14 season saw us lead the Premier League for long periods and end the campaign winning the FA Cup in dramatic style at Wembley Stadium. Aaron Ramsey's winning goal capped a fine campaign for him and for Arsenal.

During the summer, the quality of our squad was seen again at the World Cup in Brazil. Arsenal players starred for their respective national sides. The tournament ended with Germany's Mesut Özil, Per Mertesacker and Lukas Podolski crowned as Champions of the World.

Back at Emirates Stadium we have new faces in the ranks, including Chilean star Alexis Sanchez and French international Mathieu Debuchy. We hope to have an even more exciting and fruitful future.

Meanwhile, I hope you enjoy this Annual. In the pages ahead, you will find plenty to inform and entertain you. Look back over the 2013/14 season, learn about your favourite players in each position, read special features about Aaron Ramsey and Per Mertesacker, and test your wits in the quiz and puzzle pages.

I want to thank all the wonderful fans who have supported the Club year after year. I speak for everyone at Arsenal FC when I say your continuing loyalty is crucial to us. We share the credit for every victory with you and look forward to many more to come.

Thank you for your support. We hope to see you at Emirates Stadium soon!

Arsène Wenger

premier league review 2013-14

The opening month of the league campaign was one of two halves: the Gunners lost a game 3-1 and then won a game by the same margin. The first match of the month proved disappointing as the Gunners fell to defeat at the hands of Aston Villa. Emirates Stadium had erupted as Olivier Giroud swept home the opener. By full time, two goals from Benteke and one from Luna had turned the smiles into frowns.

Seven days later, Wenger's team grabbed all three points on a soaking afternoon in West London. As torrential rain descended on Craven Cottage, a prodded strike from Giroud and a longer-distance brace from Lukas Podolski ensured the visiting fans went home with sunshine in their hearts. It was a game of milestones: the Club's 300th Premier League win in London and Jack Wilshere's 100th appearance for the Club. However, the most exciting statistic was this: three points for Arsenal.

17th: Arsenal 1-3 Aston Villa (Giroud)
24th: Fulham 1-3 Arsenal (Giroud, Podolski 2)

august

september

August may have been wobbly but September was wonderful. The Gunners won all four of their league ties, including the month's opener at home to rivals Tottenham. Theo Walcott's low cross allowed the lively Giroud to stab home at the near post.

New signing Mesut Özil hit the ground running at Sunderland on his Arsenal debut. He set up Giroud's 11th-minute opener and then continued to pull the strings, creating a series of chances for his new team-mates. Ramsey scored twice in the second-half to seal another win.

Özil was again in inspired form at home to Stoke. He set up all three of Arsenal's goals in the 3-1 win. Ramsey, Mertesacker and Sagna were the grateful recipients of the German's wizardry. The win took Arsenal to the top of the league.

Ramsey was again in masterful form as Arsenal went two points clear at the top of the Premier League with a 2-1 win at Swansea. The Welshman was joined on the second-half score-sheet by Serge Gnabry, following a testing first-half at the Liberty Stadium.

1st:	Arsenal 1-0 Tottenham Hotspur (Giroud)
14th:	Sunderland 1-3 Arsenal (Giroud, Ramsey 2)
22nd:	Arsenal 3-1 Stoke City (Ramsey, Mertesacker, Sagna)
28th:	Swansea City 1-2 Arsenal (Gnabry, Ramsey)

Going into October, the Gunners were unbeaten since the opening day of the Premier League season. They maintained that record throughout the month. At the Hawthorns, West Brom tested the Gunners by taking the lead minutes before half-time. A second-half screamer from Jack Wilshere, fired home from 25 yards, levelled matters.

Wilshere struck the most memorable of Arsenal's four goals against Norwich City. Having started the move, he buried the ball following delicious one-touch interplay with Olivier Giroud and Santi Cazorla. Özil was also among the goal scorers, netting twice.

At Selhurst Park, Arsenal were again made to work hard for the points. Mikel Arteta was shown red just minutes after he had opened the scoring. It was not until Giroud's late header, from a fine Ramsey cross, that the Gunners faithful could relax. The win left Arsenal five points clear at the top of the table.

6th: **West Bromwich Albion 1-1 Arsenal (Wilshere)**

19th: **Arsenal 4-1 Norwich City (Wilshere, Özil 2, Ramsey)**

26th: **Crystal Palace 0-2 Arsenal (Arteta, Giroud)**

Could the Gunners maintain their title bid and unbeaten run against fellow frontrunners Liverpool? They could. Cazorla fired home after his header rebounded from the post and then the in-form Ramsey doubled the lead with a powerful effort from 25 yards.

At Old Trafford, Wenger's side slipped to only their second defeat of the campaign to date. Despite an impressive second-half display, the visitors were unable to overcome the first-half lead Van Persie had gifted the hosts.

At home to Southampton a fortnight later, a brace from Giroud won the tie. The first came when he forced Artur Boruc into an error, the second came from the penalty spot in the 86th minute.

It was Ramsey's turn to score twice when the Gunners travelled to Cardiff on the last day of the month. At his boyhood club, he turned in passes from Özil and Walcott respectively. In between, Mathieu Flamini had also netted, with Özil again the provider.

2nd:	Arsenal 2-0 Liverpool (Cazorla, Ramsey)
10th:	Manchester United 1-0 Arsenal
23rd:	Arsenal 2-0 Southampton (Giroud 2)
30th:	Cardiff City 0-3 Arsenal (Ramsey 2, Flamini)

Nicklas Bendtner scored his first Arsenal goal since March 11 to get a 2-0 victory against Hull City underway. The dominant Gunners doubled the lead two minutes into the second-half when the deadly combination of Ramsey and Özil combined again, with the German scoring.

When Özil broke the deadlock with just 10 minutes left on the clock against Everton, another win seemed on the cards. The German had converted Walcott's header across the goal with aplomb. However, the visitors equalised just four minutes later, through Gerard Deulofeu.

Walcott netted twice at Manchester City but the hosts were in unstoppable form. The spectacular tie ended with the Gunners well-beaten on the day but still top of the league. After nine goals in one tie there were none in the following match, as Arsenal drew 0-0 with London rivals Chelsea.

After three games without a win, Arsenal fans were treated to two victories in a row. After going 1-0 down after 46 minutes at West Ham, Wenger's team struck back with two goals from Walcott and one from the returning Poldolski.

But could the Gunners finish 2013 on top of the Premier League? They could. Midway through the second-half at St James' Park, Giroud headed home a Walcott free-kick to wrap up the three points for Wenger's side. Despite considerable pressure from the hosts, Arsenal had held firm. They would enter 2014 at the summit of English league football.

4th: Arsenal 2-0 Hull City (Bendtner, Özil)

8th: Everton 1-1 Arsenal (Özil)

14th: Manchester City 6-3 Arsenal (Walcott 2, Mertesacker)

23rd: Arsenal 0-0 Chelsea

26th: West Ham United 1-3 Arsenal (Walcott 2, Podolski)

29th: Newcastle United 0-1 Arsenal (Giroud)

It took two late, late goals for Arsenal to win the first match of 2014. On New Year's Day goals from Bendtner and Walcott, during a frantic final two minutes of the clash with Cardiff, wrapped up the points when a draw seemed so likely.

A brace of goals in the space of just 59 seconds from Wilshere and Giroud sent the Gunners back to the summit of the Premier League with a hard-fought victory at Villa Park two weeks later. Belief was growing in the camp.

At home to Fulham, Cazorla netted a memorable pair of goals to claim another win for Mr Wenger's side. The Club remained at the top of the Premier League, where they had been every week but one since the middle of September.

After going behind at Southampton, Arsenal came roaring back with second-half goals from Giroud and Cazorla. However, a minute after the Spaniard's strike, the Saints scored again and the match ended all-square.

1st:	**Arsenal 2-0 Cardiff** (Bendtner, Walcott)
13th:	**Aston Villa 1-2 Arsenal** (Wilshere, Giroud)
18th:	**Arsenal 2-0 Fulham** (Cazorla 2)
28th:	**Southampton 2-2 Arsenal** (Giroud, Cazorla)

After a strong start to the year, the Gunners faded somewhat during a packed February. However, the month began with a fine win against Crystal Palace. Oxlade-Chamberlain netted twice for the Club after a dull first-half.

At Anfield the following week, Liverpool came flying out of the traps and were 4-0 ahead within 20 minutes of the opening whistle. Despite a penalty from Arteta in the 69th minute, the Gunners were ultimately well beaten.

Manchester United were the next visitors to Emirates Stadium and arrived in determined mood. Arsenal were unable to overcome a stubborn and rigid performance from the visitors and the tie ended goalless with the points shared.

Arsenal needed a win and they got one in the final league tie of the month. Sunderland were beaten by four goals to one with Giroud the architect of Arsenal's win, netting two of the goals himself.

2nd: Arsenal 2-0 Crystal Palace
(Oxlade-Chamberlain 2)

8th: Liverpool 5-1 Arsenal
(Arteta, pen)

12th: Arsenal 0-0 Manchester United

22nd: Arsenal 4-1 Sunderland
(Giroud 2, Rosicky, Koscielny)

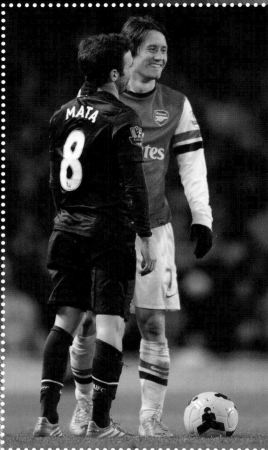

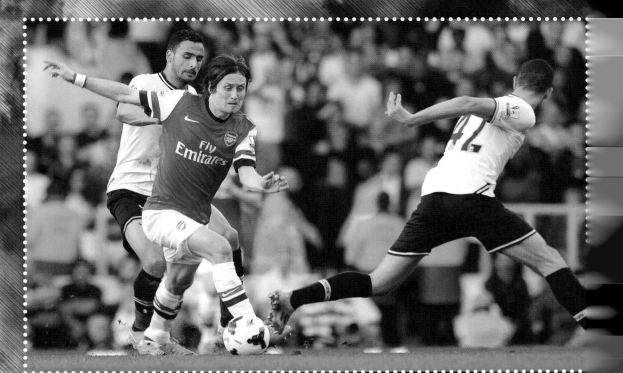

march

March proved to be a testing month for Arsenal. It began with defeat at Stoke City. A closely-fought tie was decided from the penalty spot, after Koscielny handled in the area.

A thundering, second-minute goal from Rosicky was just the medicine Arsenal needed in their next tie – against local rivals Tottenham Hotspur. This result meant the Gunners had beaten Spurs in all three of their meetings during 2013/14, failing to concede a goal in any of them.

The next London derby was a less enjoyable occasion. Arsenal lost 6-0 to a rampant Chelsea. As the 10-man Gunners were so soundly beaten, it was forgotten that this was Mr Wenger's 1,000th game in charge of the Club.

With just seconds to go against Swansea three days later, it seemed that goals from Podolski and Giroud had earned a much-needed home win. However, a last-gasp own goal from Flamini meant the Gunners had to settle for just one point.

In the next tie, the honours again ended even. However, this time Flamini was on the score-sheet at the right end, netting against Manchester City. March had been a strong reminder of how competitive the Premier League is.

1st:	**Stoke City 1-0 Arsenal**
16th:	**Tottenham Hotspur 0-1 Arsenal (Rosicky)**
22nd:	**Chelsea 6-0 Arsenal**
25th:	**Arsenal 2-2 Swansea (Podolski, Giroud)**
29th:	**Arsenal 1-1 Manchester City (Flamini)**

The return of Welsh wizard Aaron Ramsey was a bright spot during a challenging afternoon at Goodison Park. The 3-0 defeat by Everton dealt a blow to the Club's bid for the Premier League title.

A brace of goals from Podolski and a sublime strike from Giroud eased the Gunners to a welcome victory over the Hammers in the middle of the month. The fact the Reds had recovered after initially going 1-0 down showed their character at its best.

Suddenly, things were looking brighter. Two goals from Podolski and one from the ever-convincing Ramsey strengthened the Gunners' position in the top four and boosted confidence among all who love the Club.

Close-range strikes from Özil and Koscielny were the backbone of a welcome win over Newcastle United. Giroud added a third in the second-half, converting a cross from Özil, who had been magnificently influential all evening. As the London Underground slowed to a standstill, the Gunners were motoring well.

6th:	Everton 3-0 Arsenal
15th:	Arsenal 3-1 West Ham United (Podolski 2, Giroud)
20th:	Hull City 0-3 Arsenal (Ramsey, Podolski 2)
28th:	Arsenal 3-0 Newcastle United (Kosicielny, Özil, Giroud)

maY

By the time the Gunners took to the field against West Brom, a fourth-place finish had been confirmed by results elsewhere. A first-half strike from Giroud sealed the three points that boosted confidence with the FA Cup Final approaching.

Then, in the final league match of the season, Mr Wenger's side beat Norwich 2-0 at Carrow Road. Aaron Ramsey opened the scoring in the 53rd minute, with Carl Jenkinson scoring his first for the Club nine minutes later.

At the end of a thrilling league campaign, Arsenal finished just seven points off top spot. Having been at the top of the table for much of the campaign, the Gunners showed they have the ability to lead the way in Europe's most exciting league. Optimism is high for the future.

4th: Arsenal 1-0 West Bromwich Albion (Giroud)
11th: Norwich City 0-2 Arsenal
(Ramsey, Jenkinson)

V STOKE CITY

AARON'S MAGIC MOMENTS
How Ramsey rules the roost

Having scored twice in Turkey, the Welsh wonder scored twice during the return tie against Fenerbahce in August. The pick of the pair was his second. After great work from Gibbs on the left, Ramsey fired the full-back's cross into the far corner of the net.

In September, Aaron opened the scoring against Stoke City at Emirates Stadium. Just five minutes in, Özil's free-kick was spilled by Asmir Begovic for Rambo to score. The German and Welshman would prove a deadly combination throughout the campaign.

In the meantime, Aaron was named the Barclays Player of the Month and Arsenal Player of the Month.

V LIVERPOOL

V NORWICH

Against Norwich in October, Aaron was in impish mood. The crowning glory of his skilful afternoon was his goal in the 83rd minute. He weaved one way and then the other in the box, taking the Canaries defence out of the game, and then fired home. Five minutes later he set up Özil to make it 4-1.

Going five points clear at the top of the table after beating Liverpool was a great feeling. Doing so thanks to a Ramsey wonder strike felt even better. After 59 minutes at Emirates Stadium, he collected the ball 25 yards from goal, teed himself up and smashed a volley over Mignolet and just under the bar.

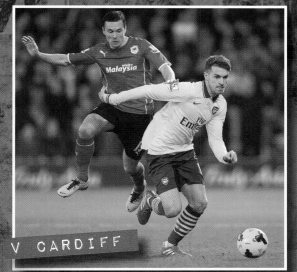

V CARDIFF

Aaron showed he is a classy guy as well as a classy player when the Gunners travelled to his old club, Cardiff. He received a fond reception on his return to South Wales and returned the love by choosing not to celebrate either of his goals.

The Ramsey-Özil combination was deadly again in December. A few minutes into the second-half against Hull City, the Welshman conjured up a chance for the German to score. This was far from the last time Hull would hear from Rambo during the campaign.

In March, Aaron signed a new, long-term deal with the Club. After inking the new contract, he looked into the future and said: "I feel like there's plenty more to come".

Ramsey was the bane of Hull again in April. He opened the scoring in the league clash at the KC Stadium, completing a fine move involving Özil and Cazorla with a clinical strike.

The following month, the Welshman was the scourge of Hull once more. After the Gunners fell behind 2-0 in the FA Cup final, Ramsey completed the comeback with a stabbed extra-time winner. He made it look easy but it was a tricky strike at a tense time. At the final whistle he became emotional as he looked back over a momentous campaign.

RAMSEY HOLDS THE CUP ALOFT

AFTER THE FA CUP FINAL

FA Cup Review

Arsenal reached – and ultimately won – the FA Cup final without leaving North London. The Club's campaign in the cup that cheers was one of drama involving a North London derby, penalties galore and even a power cut. Throughout, Mr Wenger's boys remained composed and magnificent. Here is how the Club reached the final hurdle of the famous competition.

3RD ROUND: HOME v TOTTENHAM HOTSPUR

First up, it was North London derby time for the Gunners. Santi Cazorla was the orchestrator of a virtuoso performance. It was the Spaniard who opened the scoring in the 32nd minute. Gnabry fed Santi on the left and the Spaniard crashed home his second goal of the campaign. In the 62nd minute, Rosicky capitalised on a moment of indecision from Rose and surged forward before clipping home a wonderful finish.

MATCH FACT:

With nine minutes left. Theo Walcott picked up an injury, meaning the Gunners had to complete the tie with just 10 men.

4TH ROUND: HOME v COVENTRY CITY

Two first-half goals from Lukas Podolski gave the Gunners a fine cushion going into the interval. The second was the pick of the strikes: Gnabry's corner was headed on by Mertesacker for Podolski to send home a header. That had been an all-German affair but in the second-half it was a Frenchman and a Spaniard on the score-sheet. Giroud scored within five minutes of coming on as a substitute and then Cazorla crowned the victory.

MATCH FACT

Gunners substitute Gedion Zelalem, 16, became the first player to feature for Arsenal who was born after Wenger took charge of the Club.

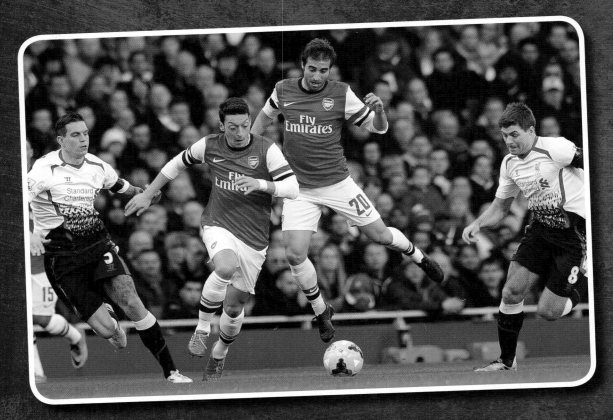

5TH ROUND: HOME v LIVERPOOL

Despite a lively opening from Liverpool, the Gunners emerged victorious from this tie. In the 16th minute, Özil found Sanogo, who controlled the ball and fired a powerful shot, which hit Gerrard and rebounded for Oxlade-Chamberlain to shoot home from close quarters. Then, after 47 minutes, Oxlade-Chamberlain sped down the right flank and found Podolski who slammed home his sixth goal of the season.

MATCH FACT:

Steven Gerrard's consolation strike was the first goal Arsenal had conceded at Emirates in 695 minutes.

QUARTER-FINAL: HOME v EVERTON

For the second round running, Wenger's team came up against opponents from Merseyside – and, once again, the Gunners were triumphant. Özil was first on the score-sheet, stroking home a perfectly weighted pass from Cazorla. After an equaliser from Everton, Arteta scored a twice-taken penalty after 70 minutes. Then, in the last 10 minutes, Olivier Giroud put the tie beyond the visitor's reach with two goals.

MATCH FACT:

The last time Arsenal were drawn at home for the first four rounds of the competition was in 1950.

SEMI-FINAL: WEMBLEY v WIGAN

The semi-final v Wigan was a tricky affair. It took 120 minutes of football and then a tense penalty shoot-out for the match to be decided in Arsenal's favour. Wigan opened the scoring on 63 minutes, with Gomez converting a penalty after Mertesacker had felled Callum McManaman. It was Big Per who scored the equaliser, though, guiding in a close-range header from a wild shot by Alex Oxlade-Chamberlain. After extra time, the penalty shoot-out saw Fabianski save from Gary Caldwell and Jack Collison. The winning penalty was scored by Cazorla.

MATCH FACT:

This victory set up Arsenal's first FA Cup final appearance since 2005.

The FA Cup Final

ARSENAL 3-2 WEMBLEY v HULL CITY, MAY 17, 2014

(Cazorla 17, Koscielny 72, Ramsey 109)
Attendance: 89,345

The eleventh FA Cup final win in Arsenal's history was a sweet moment for the Club – but it did not come easily. On a day of drama at Wembley Stadium the Gunners fell two goals behind in the opening nine minutes and came back to win 3-2.

A strike apiece from Hull's two centre-backs, James Chester and Curtis Davies, gave Arsenal a mountain to climb. Santi Cazorla started the fightback with a 17th-minute goal from a sweet free-kick.

It was not until deep into the second-half that Arsenal drew level. Laurent Koscielny, who was a colossus throughout the fightback, scrambled the ball home from close range, setting-up half an hour of extra time.

By now the Gunners were in dominant form. Some shrewd substitutions from Mr Wenger had revitalised the team and it seemed only a matter of time before the Gunners would take the lead.

They did just that through Aaron Ramsey, who stabbed home a near-post drive after a fine flick from Olivier Giroud.

With just minutes left, Lukasz Fabianski caused the Gunners faithful a moment of panic when he charged out of his area after Mertesacker slipped. Thankfully, Sone Aluko fired wide from the tight angle.

At the final whistle the Arsenal players, coaching team and fans united in an eruption of immense joy. Arsenal had won the FA Cup!

> 66 It was mind-blowing. I have dreamt about this day for many years as a young kid coming through and it hasn't quite sunk in yet. 99

Aaron Ramsey

ARSENAL TEAM

21	Fabianski
3	Sagna
6	Koscielny
4	Mertesacker
28	Gibbs
8	Arteta
19	Cazorla (Rosicky 105)
16	Ramsey
11	Özil (Wilshere 105)
9	Podolski (Sanogo 61)
12	Giroud

Substitutes

1	Szczesny
5	Vermaelen
17	Monreal
7	Rosicky
10	Wilshere
20	Flamini
22	Sanogo

10 goals of the season

TOMAS ROSICKY V TOTTENHAM (MAR)

Bursting through the Spurs half, Rosicky swapped a pass with Oxlaide-Chamberlain before curling the ball into the far corner with his right foot.

TOMAS ROSICKY V SUNDERLAND (FEB)

The goalscorer was also intimately involved in the build up to this strike. Having exchanged several passes with his colleagues, he lifted it over the advancing goalkeeper.

AARON RAMSEY V NORWICH (OCT)

The Welshman created this goal and scored it. He weaved his way through the box before firing home an unstoppable shot.

THEO WALCOTT V MAN CITY (DEC)

Aaron Ramsey lifted the ball into the path of Walcott who chipped it into the far corner of the net.

AARON RAMSEY V HULL CITY (MAY)

The goal that won the FA Cup for Arsenal. Giroud flicked the ball into the path of the lively Welshman who stabbed it home.

JACK WILSHERE V NORWICH (OCT)

Breathtaking interplay between Cazorla, Giroud and the young Englishman resulted in a goal to remember from Wilshere.

SANTI CAZORLA V HULL CITY (MAY)

With the Gunners 2-0 down at Wembley, the pressure was on. Cazorla curled in a peach of a free-kick to begin the fightback.

AARON RAMSEY V LIVERPOOL (NOV)

Özil sent a weighted pass through to the Welshman who controlled it, composed himself and then volleyed the ball into the back of the net. His 10th goal of the season was a joy.

MESUT OZIL V NAPOLI (OCT)

Ramsey burst forward and unleashed a fantastic cross which the German converted beautifully.

OLIVIER GIROUD V WEST HAM (APRIL)

With a long pass floating into a crowded box, it seemed only a stroke of luck could see it converted. But the Frenchman opted for a stroke of genius, controlling the ball deftly before finding the net.

KNOW YOUR HISTORY!

Fun facts from Arsenal's past.

Above: Arsenal's leading appearance-maker is David O'Leary. The Irishman represented Arsenal on 722 occasions.

Below: In the 1997/98 double year, Dennis Bergkamp won both major Player of the Year awards to go with his Premier League and FA Cup medals.

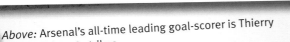

Above: Arsenal's all-time leading goal-scorer is Thierry Henry, with 228 strikes.

Below: When Gunners stars Patrick Vieira and Emmanuel Petit combined to score the third goal in France's World Cup final win over Brazil in 1998, the following morning's Daily Mirror ran the front-page headline: 'Arsenal win the World Cup!'

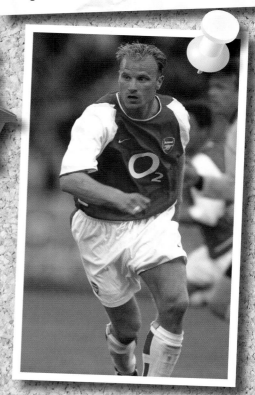

Above: The Club was the first to have a league game covered on radio (against Sheffield United in 1927), the first to have a match broadcast live on television (against Arsenal Reservers in 1937); and the first club to score in an FA Cup final staged outside England (v Liverpool in 2001 in Cardiff).

Right: When the official Club website named the 50 greatest players to represent Arsenal, the top five were: 1) Thierry Henry; 2) Dennis Bergkamp; 3) Tony Adams; 4) Ian Wright; 5) Patrick Vieira.

Below: Tony Adams.

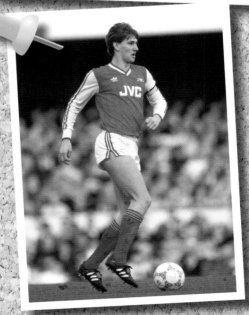

UEFA Champions League Review

Fenerbahce v Arsenal 21/8/13

In the second-half of their visit to Turkey the Gunners as good as sealed their passage into the Champions League group stages. Walcott crossed for Gibbs to open the scoring, his first European goal for the Club. Just after the hour, Ramsey surged through midfield and fired home to double the lead. Giroud's late penalty made it three.

Fenerbahce 0-3 Arsenal (Gibbs, Ramsey, Giroud)

EURO FACT: This was not the first time Ramsey had scored against Fenerbahce. The Welshman scored his first Gunners goal against them, way back in 2008.

Arsenal v Fenerbahce 27/8/13

Having pulled the strings in the first leg, Ramsey scored twice back at Emirates Stadium. The Welsh wonder scored in each half, to quash any hope the visitors had of mounting a comeback. His volley 18 minutes from time handed Arsenal a 5-0 aggregate victory. The Club had reached the group stages of the Champions League for the 14th successive season.

Arsenal 2-0 Fenerbahce (Ramsey 2)

EURO FACT: This win meant the Gunners maintained their 100% record in Champions League qualifiers – 12 games, 12 wins – and also racked up a third victory inside seven days.

Marseille v Arsenal 18/9/13

Second-half strikes from Walcott and Ramsey sealed the win for Mr Wenger's side in the Champions League group opener at Stade Velodrome. Despite a last-minute penalty from the hosts, Arsenal were always in command once they had taken the lead. The pick of the goals came from Walcott: he converted a Gibbs cross with aplomb to lash the ball home.

Marseille 1-2 Arsenal (Walcott, Ramsey)

EURO FACT: This was the Club's 10th consecutive away win.

Arsenal v Napoli 1/10/13

The Gunners celebrated the 17th anniversary of Mr Wenger's appointment as manager by beating the Italians and taking control of Group F. Early goals from Özil and Giroud had the visitors deflated just 15 minutes into the tie. The German's strike was his first for the Club and the celebrations on and off the pitch showed the plentiful affection that exists for the record signing.

Arsenal 2-0 Napoli (Özil, Giroud)

EURO FACT: This was the first match the Italians had lost all season.

Arsenal v Borussia Dortmund
22/10/13

The Gunners deserved more from this tie. The Germans took the lead through Henrikh Mkhitaryan, before Giroud thumped home the equaliser from close-range, four minutes before the interval. But a late winner from Robert Lewandowski left the Gunners empty-handed at the end of the tie. They remained top of the group but qualification was now in the balance.

Arsenal 1-2 Borussia Dortmund (Giroud)

EURO FACT: The match took place on Arsene Wenger's 64th birthday

Borussia Dortmund
v Arsenal 6/11/13

The Gunners grabbed a massive victory in Germany, thanks to Aaron Ramsey's second-half goal. During the first-half, the Germans were in dominant and threatening form, as had been predicted. But the Welshman's 62nd minute header, converting a cross from the shrewd Özil, turned the tide in favour of Mr Wenger's wonderboys.

Borussia Dortmund 0-1 Arsenal (Ramsey)

EURO FACT: Some 3,300 Gunners fans travelled to Germany to cheer on their heroes

Arsenal v Marseille 26/11/13

The Gunners eased closer to qualification thanks to a pair of goals from Jack Wilshere. The popular midfielder curled in his first after just 30 seconds and stabbed home another midway through the second half. The goals ensured that Arsenal fended off a Marseille side who had struggled to find their feet in this competition.

Arsenal 2-0 Marseille (Wilshere 2)

EURO FACT: This was the first time Jack Wilshere had scored two goals in one match.

Napoli v Arsenal 11/12/13

This tie saw Arsenal qualify from the group despite a 2-0 defeat. The visitors went behind to an expert finish from Gonzalo Higuain 16 minutes from time in the Stadio Sao Paolo. Mikel Arteta was dismissed a few minutes later, setting up a nervous finale. Although José Callejon put the Gunners two behind with the final kick of the game, Mr Wenger's team went through.

Napoli 2-0 Arsenal

EURO FACT: The result meant the Gunners reached the knockout stages of the Champions League for the 14th successive season.

Arsenal v Bayern Munich 19/2/14

Arsenal were left with a mountainous task after losing 2-0 to the German giants in the first-leg of this knockout tie. For the second year running, the two sides met in this stage. Second-half goals from Toni Kroos and Thomas Muller meant Bayern again emerged triumphant from the opening battle. However, in the previous season the Gunners had won in Germany. Did the Emirates faithful dare to dream?

Arsenal 0-2 Bayern Munich

EURO FACT: This tie was Yaya Sanogo's first start in the competition.

Bayern Munich v Arsenal 11/3/14

The Gunners bowed out of the Champions League with elegance and dignity. This draw in Germany was all the more impressive for the fact that, when Bastian Schweinsteiger scored just after the break, putting the tie beyond Arsenal, they continued to press forward. Their determined spirit was rewarded by a goal from Podolski after 57 minutes. However, it was the holders who went through.

Bayern Munich 1-1 Arsenal (Podolski)

EURO FACT: In the last five years the Gunners have been drawn twice against both Bayern and Barcelona in the knockout stage.

Podolski, Mertesacker & Özil

Arsenal at the World Cup!

How the Gunners fared at football's biggest tournament

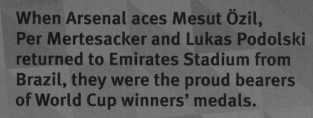

When Arsenal aces Mesut Özil, Per Mertesacker and Lukas Podolski returned to Emirates Stadium from Brazil, they were the proud bearers of World Cup winners' medals.

The German trio were part of the squad that romped all the way to the final, beating Argentina 1-0 in Rio de Janeiro. Poignantly, for Gunners fans, Özil was replaced by Mertesacker in the final minute of extra time. As the Germans paraded at the end of the game, Podolski's ever-present smile was bigger than ever.

All three men had played an important part in the eventual winners' campaign. Lukas made two cameo appearances over 53 minutes and Per lined up on five occasions. Mesut featured in every game for Germany and was on the score-sheet against Algeria.

Alexis Sanchez, just weeks away from his move to the Club, was also a star of the tournament. He was an ever-present for Chile, scoring against Australia and Brazil.

The other Gooners to score in Brazil were Olivier Giroud, who hit the net for France against Switzerland and Joel Campbell who banged in a beauty for Costa Rica against Uruguay.

Joel Campbell

Alexis Sanchez

George Eastham

Johan Djourou

The Magnificent Seven!

Seven players have won the World Cup while at Arsenal. George Eastham (England 1966); Patrick Vieira and Emmanuel Petit (France 1998); Cesc Fabregas (Spain 2010); Mesut Özil, Per Mertesacker, Lukas Podolski (Germany 2014).

Emmanuel Petit & Patrick Viera

Olivier Giroud

Here is a full list of Arsenal players' appearances in Brazil:

Joel Campbell (Costa Rica) – 3

Jack Wilshere (England) – 2

Olivier Giroud (France) – 5

Laurent Koscielny (France) – 4

Mesut Özil (Germany) – 7

Per Mertesacker (Germany) – 6

Lukas Podolski (Germany) – 2

Santi Cazorla (Spain) – 2

Johan Djourou (Switzerland) – 2

Alexis Sanchez (Chile) – 4

Santi Cazorla

Capital One Cup Review

Although the Club's Capital One Cup campaign was a short one, as ever there was drama to be witnessed and experience to be drawn. Here is the lowdown.

West Brom v Arsenal

It took a penalty shoot-out to settle the opening tie of Arsenal's Capital One Cup campaign. Thomas Eisfeld gave the Gunners the lead just after the hour mark at the Hawthorns. He unleashed a composed strike from Nicklas Bendtner's assist. However, after West Brom equalised, the tie went to a penalty shoot-out. Nacho Monreal scored the winning spot-kick, sending the Gunners through to the next round.

25 September, 2013, WBA 1-1 Arsenal (Arsenal won 4-3 on penalties); (Eisfeld, 62)

Arsenal v Chelsea

Both teams fielded stronger sides than expected for this tie. Ultimately, the Blues were to prevail. The hosts had their chances, with Monreal, Cazorla and Ramsey all coming close for Arsenal. Later in the game, substitute Olivier Giroud tested Mark Schwarzer, with Jack Wilshere also enjoying a chance. But it was Chelsea who put their chances away. In doing so, they ended the Club's involvement in the competition for another year.

29 October, 2013, Arsenal 0-2 Chelsea

Arsenal's League Cup Victories

1987: Arsenal 2-1 Liverpool

Having beaten Spurs in the semi-final, the Gunners defeated Liverpool in the Wembley final. Until this tie, Liverpool had never lost a game in any competition in which Ian Rush scored. Charlie Nicholas' winner ended that record and won the cup for the Arsenal.

1993: Arsenal 2-1 Sheffield Wednesday

The Gunners won the League Cup thanks to goals from Ian Wright and Steve Morrow. Arsenal also won the FA Cup this season, with Sheffield Wednesday the opponents in that competition's final too. It was the first time a team had won both domestic cups in the same season.

20 FACTS ABOUT PER MERTESACKER!

1. Standing at six feet and six inches, he is the tallest player ever to represent Arsenal.

2. During a trip to Britain as a 10-year-old, Per bought a replica Arsenal shirt. After joining the Gunners in 2011, he said: "I am delighted to finally get to play at a team I always supported."

3. He credits his father for guiding his passion for football from the start. "My father was my coach and mentor," he says.

4. Per's first club as a player was Hannover 96.

5. From early in his career, the German tabloids described him as 'the defence pole' (die Abwehrlatte).

6. He is a fan of the music of a German DJ called Paul Kalkbrenner.

15. The couple, who married in 2013, now have two children.

16. Per has a lot of adrenaline in his body after matches. He says that sometimes, after a night match, he cannot sleep until 5am.

17. Big Per says he finds English food a bit "different".

18. Arsenal is the third side Mertesacker has lined-up alongside Mesut Özil for. The duo have also played alongside each other for Werder Bremen and, of course, Germany.

19. At the FA Cup victory parade the German colossus led the Gunners faithful in a heartfelt chant of 'Arsenal till I die.'

20. He scored twice at Wembley during the 2013/14 season: for Germany against England in November, and for Arsenal against Wigan in the FA Cup semi-final.

7. Per received praise in Germany when he went 31 games without a booking following his Bundesliga debut.

8. He made his international debut for Germany as a 20 year old in 2004. The opponents were Iran.

9. In 2006 he founded the 'Per-Mertesacker-Stiftung' - a charitable foundation that helps support amateur sportsmen and the poor. "I try to put something back." he said.

10. He won a runners-up medal at the 2008 European Championships.

11. As a teenager he grew so fast that he suffered knee problems which sidelined him from a lot of games. He believes the experience gave him a wider perspective on life.

12. An ankle injury denied him the opportunity to appear in the Werder Bremen team for the 2009 German Cup and Uefa Cup finals.

13. His brother Timo, who closely resembles Per, sometimes travels to away fixtures on Arsenal fans' coaches. "He doesn't introduce himself as my brother," says Per. "He just badly wants an adventure."

14. As well as football, Per is a fan of basketball and handball. His wife, Ulrike Stange, has represented Germany in the latter sport.

CROSSWORD

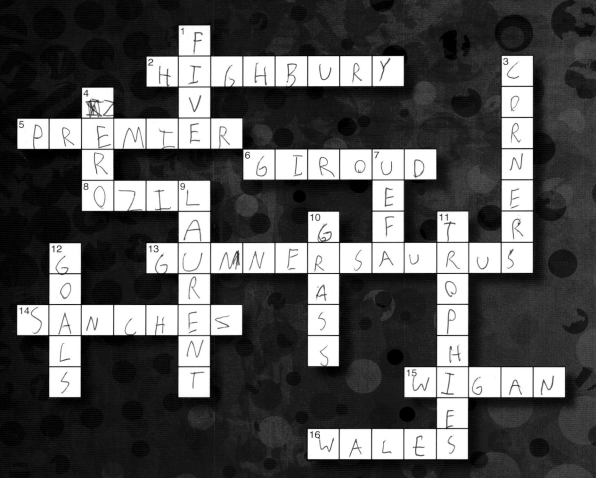

Across

2 The Club's former home was known as _____ . (8)

5 The name of England's top division. (7)

6 Our star striker throughout 2013/14 was Olivier _____ . (6)

8 The surname of the record signing who arrived from Real Madrid in 2013. (4)

13 The name of the Club mascot. (12)

14 Arsenal's July 2014 signing from Barcelona, Alexis _____ . (7)

15 The team the Gunners faced in the FA Cup semi-final was _____ Athletic. (5)

16 What country does Aaron Ramsey represent? (5)

Down

1 How many goals did both teams combined score in the FA Cup final? (4)

3 There are four of these on every pitch. (7)

4 How many goals did Arsenal concede against Spurs during the 2013/14 season? (4)

7 Which body governs European football? (4)

9 The first name of our French centre back who joined in 2010. (7)

10 It's not always greener on the other side. (5)

11 Arsenal enjoy winning these. (8)

12 It helps to get more of these than your opponents. (5)

Answers on Page 61

SPOT THE BALL!

Can you work out which is the real ball in the picture below?

Answer on Page 61

Player Profiles

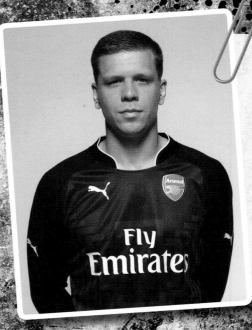

Wojciech Szczęsny

With over 150 appearances under his belt, Wojciech is now an established figure in the Arsenal team. Goalkeeping is in the blood: Wojciech's father Maciej kept goal for Poland. He was a star throughout the 2013/14 campaign, helping Arsenal to keep a total of 24 clean sheets in all competitions for the 13/14 season.

The Lowdown

Born:	April 18, 1990, Warsaw, Poland
Position:	Goalkeeper
Squad Number:	1
Previous Clubs:	Legia Warsaw, Brentford (loan)
Arsenal Debut:	September 22, 2009

Laurent Koscielny

An athletic and alert defender, Laurent is also a superb reader of the game. While his equaliser in the FA Cup final changed the course of the tie, his defensive contributions at Wembley should also be noted. A true all-rounder, the Frenchman makes pivotal contributions across the field.

The Lowdown

Born:	September 10, 1985, Tulle, France
Position:	Defender
Squad Number:	6
Previous Clubs:	En Avant Guingamp, Tours, Lorient
Arsenal Debut:	August 15, 2010

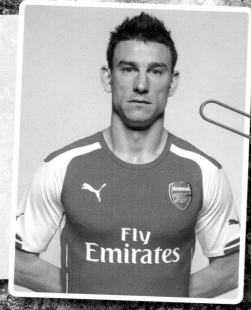

Kieran Gibbs

Prior to moving into the back four, Kieran had been a winger. This lends an effective attacking dimension to the play of this solid defender. Since his debut in 2007, 'Gibbo' has won an army of Arsenal fans. He made a key contribution to the FA Cup win, clearing a Hull effort off the line.

The Lowdown

Born:	September 26, 1989, Lambeth, London
Position:	Defender
Squad Number:	3
Previous Clubs:	Wimbledon, Norwich City
Arsenal Debut:	October 31, 2007

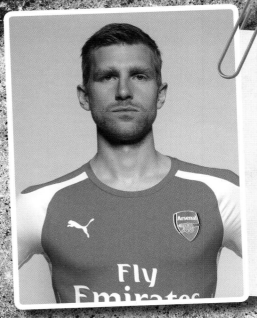

Per Mertesacker

Committed, controlling and commanding – the giant German has become a firm favourite of the Gunners faithful. His partnership with Laurent Koscielny flourished throughout 2013/14. Per also chipped in some crucial goals, particularly his late equaliser in the FA Cup semi-final against Wigan. The 6ft6in defender returned from the summer break a world champion.

The Lowdown

Born:	September 29, 1984, Hannover, Germany
Position:	Defender
Squad Number:	4
Previous Clubs:	Werder Bremen, Hannover 96
Arsenal Debut:	September 10, 2011

Nacho Monreal

The Spanish international joined the Gunners at the end of the 2012/13 winter transfer window. He adapted with ease to the bustle of the Premier League, proving a committed defender with exciting attacking aspirations. In his first full season with the Club he scored the winning penalty in the Capital One Cup shoot-out against West Brom, a standout moment in a season of contributions.

The Lowdown

Born:	February 26, 1986, Pamplona, Spain
Position:	Defender
Squad Number:	18
Previous Clubs:	Osasuna, Malaga
Arsenal Debut:	February 02, 2013

Mesut Özil

The German maestro joined the Club in a record deal in September 2013 and immediately set about inspiring the team to new heights. As well as making his own incisive contributions, Mesut worked as a talisman, encouraging those around him. His relationship with Aaron Ramsey proved particularly fruitful.

The Lowdown

Born:	October 15, 1988. Gelsenkirchen, Germany
Position:	Midfielder
Squad Number:	11
Previous Clubs:	Schalke, Werder Bremen, Real Madrid
Arsenal Debut:	14 September, 2013

Jack Wilshere

A player of vision, grace and steel, Jack has been a firm favourite among Gunners fans since his debut six years ago. He has been a mainstay of midfield as faces have changed around him. Jack was unfortunate to be injured in the build-up to the FA Cup final yet he still managed a substitute appearance which helped change the game.

The Lowdown

Born:	January 01, 1992, Stevenage, Hertfordshire
Position:	Midfielder
Squad Number:	10
Previous Clubs:	Bolton
Arsenal Debut:	September 13, 2008

Mikel Arteta (C)

The Spaniard was already a familiar Premier League face when he joined Arsenal in 2011, having made over 200 appearances for Everton. The former Barcelona and Rangers star is a solid, deep-lying midfielder who nonetheless chips in with goals, including from the penalty spot. Mikel is the 2014/15 Club Captain.

The Lowdown

Born:	March 26, 1982, San Sebastian, Spain
Position:	Midfielder
Squad Number:	8
Previous Clubs	Everton, Real Sociedad, Rangers, PSG (loan), Barcelona
Arsenal Debut:	September 10, 2011

Tomas Rosicky

When the Gunners frolicked on the Wembley turf having won the FA Cup, none looked happier than Tomas. The courageous, energetic attacking midfielder has been with the Club for eight years and was delighted to finally get his hands on some silverware. He has previously won trophies in Germany and Czech Republic.

The Lowdown

Born	October 04, 1980, Prague, Czech Republic
Position:	Midfielder
Squad Number:	7
Previous Clubs	Borussia Dortmund, Sparta Prague, CKD Kompresory
Arsenal Debut	August 09, 2006

Aaron Ramsey

The Welshman was voted player of the season by the Arsenal fans for 2013/14 - and no wonder. Despite a lengthy layoff through injury midway through the campaign, he was sensational. Finding the net 16 times in 30 games, he was unstoppable all over the pitch. The crowning glory of his – and the Club's – season came at Wembley, when he netted the FA Cup final winner against Hull City.

The Lowdown

Born:	December 26, 1990, Caerphilly, Wales
Position:	Midfielder
Squad Number:	16
Previous Clubs:	Cardiff City (loan), Nottingham Forest (loan), Cardiff City
Arsenal Debut:	August 13, 2008

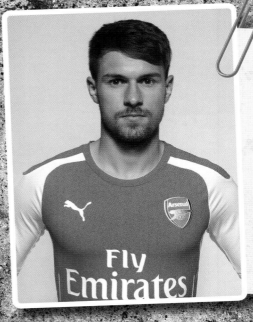

Santi Cazorla

When he picked up the man of the match award for his Arsenal debut in 2012, Santi set the bar high for himself. The Spaniard has more than lived up to the expectation that aroused. During his second season with the Club he started 41 games and scored seven goals. These included a cracker against Liverpool and the all-important free-kick against Hull City in the FA Cup Final.

The Lowdown

Born:	December 13, 1984, Llanera, Spain
Position:	Midfielder
Squad Number:	19
Previous Clubs:	Malaga, Villarreal, Recreativo, Villarreal, Oviedo
Arsenal Debut:	August 18, 2012

Gedion Zelalem

When Gedion made his first-team debut against Coventry in 2014, he was the first player to feature for Arsenal who was born after Arsène Wenger took charge. Gedion is agile and intelligent, bewitching opponents and delighting team-mates with his bright play in the middle of the park. Formerly of Hertha Berlin, Gedion has a bright future ahead of him.

The Lowdown

Born:	January 26, 1997, Berlin, Germany
Position:	Midfielder
Squad Number:	35
Previous Clubs:	Hertha Berlinr
Arsenal Debut:	24 January 2014

Francis Coquelin

Fast, feisty, yet composed, Francis debuted for the first team in the 6-0 Carling Cup win over Sheffield United in September 2008. He has since made impressive appearances in all competitions for the Club. A versatile and wholehearted youngster, he has grown in confidence and stature thanks to a loan spell in the French league.

The Lowdown

Born:	May 13, 1991, Laval, France
Position:	Midfielder
Squad Number:	34
Previous Club:	Freiberg (loan), Lorient (loan)
Arsenal Debut:	September 23, 2008

Abou Diaby

On his day, the French midfielder is one of the Premier League's finest midfield talents. Sadly, a series of injuries have robbed Abou of the opportunity to make the sort of impact that his talent and commitment deserve. He returned from a lengthy cruciate knee ligament injury in 2014. He, and everyone at the Club, look forward to a bright future for a player with great potential.

The Lowdown

Born:	May 11, 1986, Paris, France
Position:	Midfielder
Squad Number:	24
Previous Club:	Auxerre, Paris Saint-Germain
Arsenal Debut:	January 21, 2006

Mathieu Flamini

Now in his second spell with the Club, Mathieu is a committed, organised and formidable midfielder. He first joined the Gunners in 2004 from Ligue 1 side Marseille and made 153 appearances for Arsenal before joining AC Milan in the summer of 2008. He returned in the summer of 2013 and made 36 appearances in his comeback season, scoring twice.

The Lowdown

Born:	March 07, 1984, Marseille, France
Position:	Midfielder
Squad Number:	20
Previous Club:	Marseille, Arsenal, AC Milan
Arsenal Debut:	15 August, 2004

STRIKERS

Serge Gnabry

Serge made his first-team debut for Arsenal in the historic 7-5 League Cup victory away to Reading in 2012. He truly burst into the first-team the following season. The gifted attacker scored his first goal for the club in the Premier League tie against Swansea City. He went on to start eight games for the Gunners and signed a new long-term contract with the club in October 2013.

The Lowdown

Born:	July 14, 1995, Stuttgart, Germany
Position:	Striker
Squad Number:	27
Previous Clubs:	VfB Stuttgart
Arsenal Debut:	September 26, 2012

Ryo Miyaichi

The speedy Japanese winger played five times for the first team during 2013/14 and started both of the Club's Capital One Cup ties. Since signing for Arsenal in January 2011 after a successful trial period, he has benefited from loan spells in England and the Netherlands. In the latter territory the media gave him the nickname 'Ryondinho' after comparing him to Brazilian star Ronaldinho.

The Lowdown

Born:	December 14, 1992, Okazaki, Japan
Position:	Striker
Squad Number:	31
Previous Clubs:	Bolton (loan), Feyenoord (loan), Wigan Athletic (loan)
Arsenal Debut:	20 September, 2011

Olivier Giroud

The towering Frenchman proved a sturdy and determined force for Arsenal throughout the 2013/14 campaign. Often playing as a lone frontman, he led the line well and scored 22 goals, his most to date in a season. As well as scoring himself, he provided valuable assists, including Aaron Ramsey's winner in the FA Cup final.

The Lowdown

Born:	September 30, 1986, Chambery, France
Position:	Striker
Squad Number:	12
Previous Clubs:	Grenoble, Istres (loan), Tours, Montpellier
Arsenal Debut:	August 18, 2012

Theo Walcott

Theo was unlucky to pick up a serious injury against Tottenham but nothing can disguise his contribution to Arsenal over the last eight years. A speedy and intelligent player, fresh-faced Theo has notched many a goal for the Gunners, including several hat-tricks.

The Lowdown

Born:	March 16, 1989. Middlesex, England
Position:	Striker
Squad Number:	14
Previous Club:	Southampton
Arsenal Debut:	August 19, 2006

Alex Oxlade-Chamberlain

Following a path previously trodden by Theo Walcott, 'The Ox' moved from Southampton to Arsenal in 2011. A thrilling dribbler and astute passer, Alex terrified defences throughout the campaign, despite missing many games through injury. Now a fixture on the international scene, there is more to come from Alex as he matures and develops further.

The Lowdown

Born:	August 15, 1993, Portsmouth
Position:	Striker
Squad Number:	15
Previous Club:	Southampton
Arsenal Debut:	August 28, 2011

Yaya Sanogo

His four goals against Benfica in the Emirates Cup put Yaya Sanogo firmly on the football map. The energetic striker can use his physical presence to great effect. Although injury kept him out of contention for much of the 2013/14 campaign, he made significant contributions to the FA Cup ties against Liverpool and Hull City, as well as the Champions League clash with Bayern Munich.

The Lowdown

Born:	January 27, 1993, Massy, France
Position:	Striker
Squad Number:	22
Previous Club:	Auxerre
Arsenal Debut:	August 24, 2013

Joel Campbell

During the 2014 World Cup finals, Joel scored one and set up another as the Costa Rica reached the last eight of the tournament. Since joining the Gunners in 2011, he has gained valuable experience with a number of loan spells, including at Olympiacos, Lorient and Real Betis. He began the 2014/15 season hoping to show his class for the Arsenal.

The Lowdown

Born:	June 26, 1992, San José, Costa Rica
Position:	Striker
Squad Number:	28
Previous Clubs:	Olympiacos (loan), Lorient (loan), Deportivo Saprissa, Puntarenas (loan)
Arsenal Debut:	August 10, 2014 (Community Shield)

Lukas Podolski

The ever-smiling German forward never seems to need much encouragement to be happy, yet during 2013/14 his face shone more than ever. Scoring 12 goals in 20 starts, he began the campaign with a brace of strikes against Fulham. By April he had overcome injury and been named player of the month.

The Lowdown

Born:	June 04, 1985, Gliwice, Poland
Position:	Striker
Squad Number:	9
Previous Clubs:	Cologne, Bayern Munich, Cologne
Arsenal Debut:	August 18, 2012

Aaron Ramsey's FA Cup Final winner against Hull City

ODDBALL FACTS!

AARON RAMSEY'S FA Cup final winner against Hull City at Wembley sealed the club's 40th major honour overall, and the 12th under Arsène Wenger.

In matches Aaron Ramsey appeared in, the win-rate was 70.6%. In matches Aaron missed through injury, the win-rate was 55%.

The Arsenal.com Player of the Season voting went as follows: 1) **AARON RAMSEY**; 2) Per Mertesacker; 3) Laurent Koscielny.

The FA Cup final was **AARON RAMSEY'S** second: he made a substitute appearance for Cardiff City in the 2008 final against Portsmouth.

PER MERTESACKER captained the side 16 times, winning 13 (or 81%) of those games.

Arsène Wenger

Per Mertesacker

ARSÈNE WENGER is the only Arsenal manager to win the FA Cup more than once. He has now won the trophy five times.

Uniquely, the boss has won the cup in three different decades at three different venues (the old Wembley, Millennium Stadium and the new Wembley).

Laurent Koscienly

LAURENT KOSCIENLY was on the pitch for 3,974 minutes during the season.

The fifth penalty-taker against Wigan Athletic in the FA Cup semi-final would have been Bacary Sagna.

The Gunners amassed 79 points in the Premier League campaign: six more than in 2012/13.

Borussia Dortmund boss **JURGEN KLOPP** came up with the following eccentric praise for Mr Wenger: 'For me, he is Sir Arsène Wenger. I love him. He likes having the ball, playing football, passes. It's like an orchestra. But it's a silent song. I like heavy metal.'

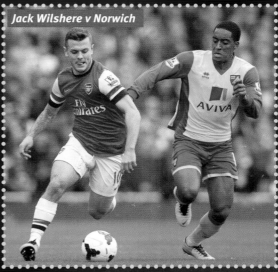

Jack Wilshere v Norwich

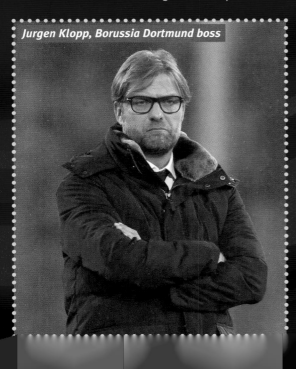

Jurgen Klopp, Borussia Dortmund boss

The Arsenal.com Goal of the Season poll voting went as follows: 1) **JACK WILSHERE** v Norwich; 2) Tomas Rosicky v Spurs; 3) Santi Cazorla v Hull City

Rosicky goal v Spurs

Arsenal beat Tottenham three times during the season – without conceding a single goal.

JUNIOR Gunners

The 30th anniversary of Junior Gunners was celebrated in style during Season 2013/14. The season was packed with loads of fun events and competitions for the young fans to enjoy.

Throughout the season, JGs and their parents were invited to Emirates Stadium to watch away matches in style. With loads of urban football challenges, arts and crafts and football freestylers, the JGs enjoyed themed Away Screenings.

Fans were also provided with behind-the-scenes access through trips to the training ground, as well as an exclusive signing session with key players.

Later in May, 400 lucky young members slept on the pitch at Emirates Stadium. The exciting event included a football session on the hallowed turf, access to loads of games, a photo session with the FA Cup trophy, and dinner in the Club Level area; A once in a lifetime experience.

Young Guns Enclosure

During Season 2013/14, the Club introduced a new seating area at selected Arsenal home games for Junior Gunners aged from 12 to 16 years old.

In this area, up to 1,000 extra discounted tickets priced at just £10 were made available for weekend Premier League category B and C home matches. Only Young Guns could sit in this section, so large groups of friends enjoyed the match together and supported their team.

At the final home match of the season, 30 lucky Junior Gunners got the chance to enjoy a football session on the pitch just after the final whistle. With the players still on the pitch, the 30 JGs had a 30-minute football session learning new tricks!

New Signings

David Ospina

Colombia international goalkeeper David Ospina signed for the Gunners from Nice in July. He began his career with Atletico Nacional, where he made 97 appearances before leaving to join Nice in 2008. The six-foot stopper made 189 league appearances during his six-year spell with the French club. Mr Wenger had tracked Ospina for some time and was thrilled to get his man.

The Lowdown

Born:	August 31, 1988, Medellin, Colombia
Position:	Goalkeeper
Squad Number:	13
Previous Clubs:	Atletico Nacional, Nice

Calum Chambers

The tall and athletic Chambers settled very quickly into the team following his transfer from Southampton. At 19 years of age and with just 22 senior matches for the Saints under his belt, he performed with poise beyond his years for Arsenal. Although he began his career in central midfield, Calum has played at both right-back and centre-back for the Saints and England youth.

The Lowdown

Born:	January 20, 1995, Petersfield, England
Position:	Defender
Squad Number:	21
Previous Clubs:	Southampton

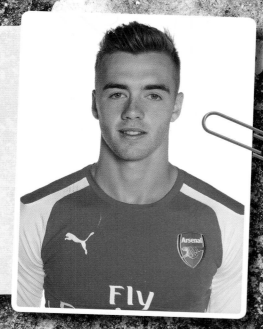

Mathieu Debuchy

The French international signed for the Club after two seasons with Newcastle United. A sturdy and attack-minded right-back, Mathieu spent the first nine years of his career with Lille. There, he won the league and cup double in 2010/11 and was named in the Ligue 1 Team of the Season the following year. He appeared in four of France's five matches at the 2014 World Cup.

The Lowdown

Born:	July 28, 1985, Fretin, France
Position:	Defender
Squad Number:	2
Previous Clubs:	Lille, Newcastle United

Alexis Sanchez

Alexis joined the Gunners in the aftermath of an impressive display at the World Cup and having scored 39 goals in 88 games for Barcelona. No wonder Arsenal fans were so thrilled. He has won a clutch of trophies including the prestigious Spanish league and Argentinian Primera Division. A committed and speedy player, he can excel in a number of attacking positions.

The Lowdown

Born:	December 19, 1988, Tocopilla, Chile
Position:	Striker
Squad Number:	17
Previous Clubs:	Cobreloa, Colo-Colo, River Plate, Udinese, Barcelona

Danny Welbeck

Danny signed for the Club From Manchester United at the end of the summer 2014 transfer window. The tall, powerful striker scored 29 goals during his impressive career at Old Trafford. A versatile talent, he is also an established England international, having won 25 England caps by the time he joined the Gunners. Welbeck adds to the growing British core at Arsenal.

The Lowdown

Born:	November 26, 1990, Manchester
Position:	Striker
Squad Number:	23
Previous Clubs:	Manchester United, Preston North End (loan), Sunderland (loan)

THE BiG ARSENAL QUIZ!

Want to put your fandom to the test? Then you came to the right place. See how many of these questions you can answer. Will you be a champion or a runner-up?

1   In which year did **Per Mertesacker** join the Club?

2   Which French side did **Yaya Sanogo** begin his career with?

3   Which side did the Gunners face in the 3rd round of the FA Cup 2013/14?

4   What nationality is former Gunners defender, now a member of the coaching staff, **Steve Bould**?

5   True or false: Two Gunners stars appeared for Germany in their opening World Cup 2014 tie, against Portugal.

6   In what year were the Gunners founded?

7   How many spells has **Mathieu Flamini** had with Arsenal?

8   Against which side did defender **Carl Jenkinson** score his first goal for the Club?

9   What nationality is **Laurent Koscielny**?

10 In which year did **Arsene Wenger** win his second double with Arsenal?

11 Name the Club's all-time top goalscorer.

12 For which Scottish side did **Mikel Arteta** play?

13 The Club have faced the same German side in two successive Champions League campaigns. Name the side.

14 Name the goalkeeper who guided Arsenal through the penalty shoot-out against Wigan Athletic.

15 What nationality is **Santi Cazorla**?

16 What was the scoreline when Arsenal played Fulham in August 2013?

17 Name the season in which Arsenal went an entire league campaign unbeaten.

18 True or false: **Theo Walcott** once played for Aberdeen.

19 Name the Gunner who scored the third goal for France in the 1998 World Cup final.

20 What nationality is **Mesut Özil**?

21 Which player came second in the Arsenal.Com 'Player of the Season' voting?

22 Who were Arsenal's penultimate Premier League opponents of the 2013/14 season?

23 Name the competition Arsenal won by beating Parma 1-0 in 1994.

24 In which year did the Club move from Highbury to Emirates Stadium: 2004 or 2006?

25 How many goals did Arsenal score in the Premier League during the 2013/14 season?

26 From which side did the Gunners sign **Aaron Ramsey**?

27 He scored the winning penalty in the FA Cup semi-final and netted from a free kick in the FA Cup final. Who is he?

28 What nationalty is **Gedion Zelalem**?

29 In which year did **Arsene Wenger** become Gunners boss: 1998 or 1996?

30 In which London borough does Arsenal FC reside?

Answers on Page 61

WORDSEARCH

See if you can find the names of 20 of Arsenal's all-time greatest players in the grid below. Words can go horizontally, vertically and diagonally.

```
R  E  W  T  J  T  Y  D  A  R  B  C  R  K
S  J  L  R  L  H  P  G  E  K  E  O  W  N
G  B  K  T  K  K  S  C  R  G  K  K  Y  Z
N  A  Z  B  S  E  F  N  J  C  R  M  R  N
I  S  D  K  A  A  D  A  M  S  R  O  N  J
N  T  J  M  O  K  C  O  K  P  D  R  E  L
N  I  A  W  S  V  L  O  M  H  U  J  H  G
E  N  M  E  R  E  E  A  R  O  K  F  W  K
J  T  R  R  A  I  K  R  L  N  A  F  V  F
D  I  Y  R  F  G  G  R  M  M  N  T  I  E
P  C  Y  B  R  L  A  H  M  A  U  Q  E  C
J  K  G  E  F  P  Y  Y  T  D  R  T  I  I
F  M  B  L  L  E  B  P  M  A  C  S  R  R
R  L  J  U  N  G  B  E  R  G  W  Z  A  K
```

Adams	Campbell	Kanu	Overmars	Rocastle
Bastin	George	Keown	Parlour	Seaman
Bergkamp	Henry	Ljungberg	Pires	Vieira
Brady	Jennings	OLeary	Rice	Wright

Answers on Page 61

58

FAMOUS FACES

See you if you can guess the 3 current Arsenal players in each of the montages below.

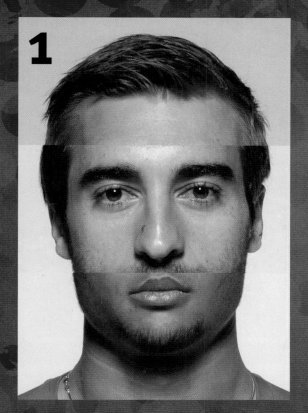

ANAGRAMS

Have a shot at unscrambling the anagrams below to reveal the names of eight Arsenal stars.

1 Social Tarzan
2 I am faint helium
3 Market creepers
4 Energy grabs

5 Charm on alone
6 Baby audio
7 Ample job cell
8 Six haze cleans

Answers on Page 61

COMPETITION!

Win a signed football shirt!

Answer the following question correctly and you could win an Arsenal FC shirt signed by a first team player.

How many goals did Thierry Henry score in his career at Arsenal?

A. 226 **B.** 249 **C.** 185.

Entry is by email only. Only one entry per contestant. Please enter **AFC SHIRT** followed by either **A, B** or **C** in the subject line of an email. In the body of the email, please include your full name, address, postcode, email address and phone number and send to: **frontdesk@ grangecommunications.co.uk** by Friday 27th March 2015.

ANSWERS

Crossword, P40

Spot the Ball, P41

The BIG Arsenal Quiz, P56

1. 2011; 2. Auxerre; 3. Tottenham Hotspur; 4. English;
5. False, it was three: Mertesacker, Özil and Podolski;
6. 1886; 7. Two; 8. Norwich City; 9. French; 10. 2002;
11. Thierry Henry; 12. Glasgow Rangers;
13. Bayern Munich; 14. Lukasz Fabianski; 15. Spanish;
16. 3-1 to Arsenal; 17. 2003/04; 18. False, he has
played for Southampton, Arsenal and England only;
19. Emmanuel Petit; 20. German; 21. Per Mertesacker;
22. West Bromwich Albion; 23. The European Cup
Winners' Cup; 24. 2006; 25. 68; 26. Cardiff City;
27. Santi Cazorla; 28. German; 29. 1996; 30. Islington

Wordsearch, P58

Famous Faces, P59

1. Per Mertesacker, Mathieu Flamini & Serge Gnabry.
2. Santi Cazorla, Theo Walcott & Aaron Ramsey.

Anagrams, P59

1. Santi Cazorla, 2. Mathieu Flamini, 3. Per Mertesacker,
4. Serge Gnabry, 5. Nacho Monreal, 6. Abou Diaby,
7. Joel Campbell, 8. Alexis Sanchez.

WHERE'S GUNNERSAURUS?

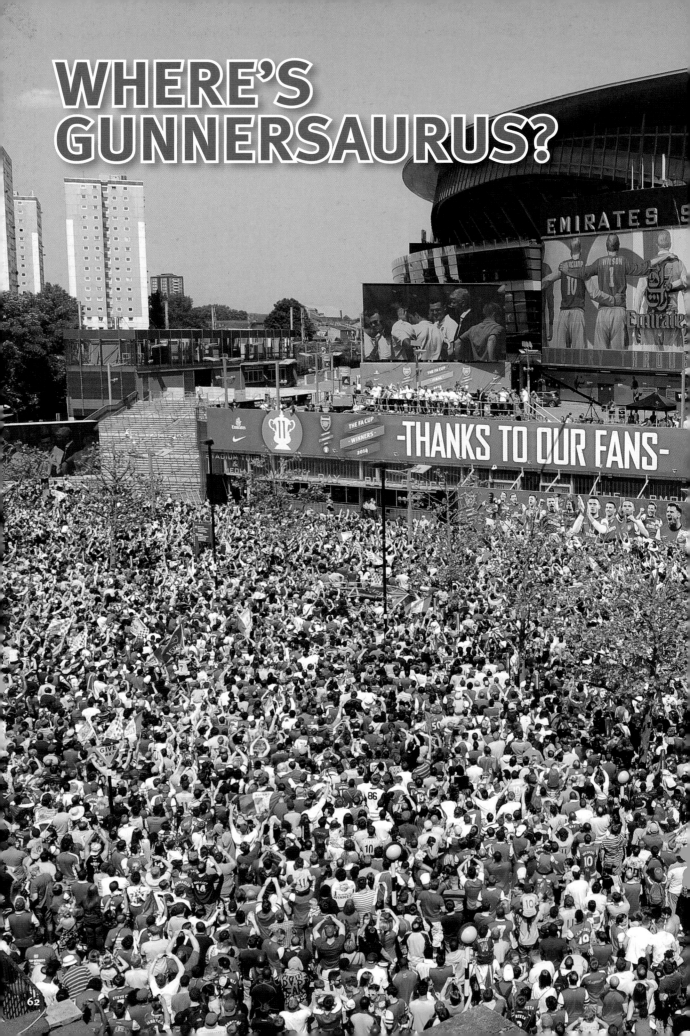